P9-DCO-774

Scholastic Success With
Writing

Grade 1

by Lisa Molengraft

S C H O L A S T I C
PROFESSIONALBOOKS

**New York • Toronto • London • Auckland • Sydney •
Mexico City • New Delhi • Hong Kong • Buenos Aires**

Scholastic Inc. grants teachers permission to photocopy the reproducible pages from this book for classroom use. No other part of this publication may be reproduced in whole or in part, or stored in a retrieval system, or transmitted in any form or by any means, electronic, mechanical, photocopying, recording, or otherwise without written permission of the publisher. For information regarding permission, write to Scholastic Inc., 557 Broadway, New York, NY 10012.

Cover art by Victoria Raymond
Cover design by Maria Lilja
Interior illustrations by Sherry Neidigh
Interior design by Quack & Company

ISBN 0-439-44494-2

Copyright © 2002 Scholastic, Inc.
All rights reserved. Printed in the U.S.A.

12   40   12 11 10

Scholastic Professional Books

Introduction

One of the greatest challenges teachers and parents face is helping children develop independent writing skills. Each writing experience is unique and individualized, making it each child's responsibility to plan, expand, and proofread his or her work. However, the high-interest topics and engaging exercises in this book will both stimulate and encourage children as they develop the necessary skills to become independent writers. This book uses these strategies to introduce grade-appropriate skills that can be used in daily writing assignments such as journals, stories, and letters. Like a stepladder, this book will help children reach the next level of independent writing.

Table of Contents

Scholastic Professional Books

Name _____

That's Amazing!

 A sentence begins with a capital letter.

 Help the mouse through the maze by coloring each box with a word that begins with a capital letter.

The	For	That	with	know	but
here	on	When	Have	next	we
as	after	good	Make	there	see
Go	Look	Are	Could	is	why
This	who	said	in	come	them
Has	Name	Before	Her	Where	The

 Read the back of a cereal box. How many capital letters did you find? Write the number next to the cheese.

Squeak!

Circle the words that show the correct way to begin each sentence.

1.  **The mouse** / **the mouse** is looking for food.

2. **he finds** / **He finds** a cracker on the floor.

3.  **he Eats** / **He eats** the cracker.

4.  **Then he** / **then He** takes a nap.

5. 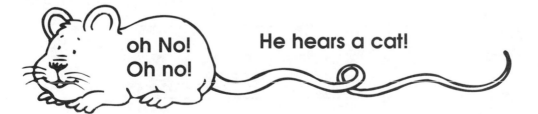 **oh No!** / **Oh no!** He hears a cat!

6.  **the Mouse** / **The mouse** runs home fast!

Scholastic Professional Books

Counting Sheep

Write the beginning words correctly to make a sentence.

1.
we read

_____ books before bed.

2.
then we

_____ hug good night.

3.
my bed

_____ is soft and cozy.

4.
my cat

_____ sleeps with me.

5.
the sky

_____ has turned dark.

6.
my eyes

_____ close.

 On another piece of paper, copy a sentence from your favorite bedtime book. Circle the capital letter at the beginning.

Scholastic Professional Books

Sweet Dreams!

Write each beginning word correctly to make a sentence.

1.  **my dog** _____ **runs in her sleep.**

2.  **she must** _____ **be dreaming.**

3.  **maybe she** _____ **is chasing a cat.**

4. 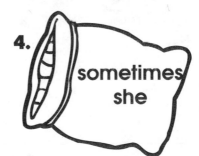 **sometimes she** _____ **even barks.**

5.  **i think** _____ **it is funny.**

 On another piece of paper, write a sentence about a dream you remember. Circle the capital letter at the beginning.

The Night Sky

 A **telling sentence** *ends with a* **period.**

period

Add a period to each sentence.

1. Many things shine in the sky at night____

2. The moon looks the brightest____

3. It is closest to Earth____

4. The stars look like tiny dots____

5. They are very far away____

6. The sun is a star____

7. Planets look like colored stars____

8. Their light does not twinkle____

9. Shooting stars look like stars that are falling____

10. There are many things to see in the night sky____

Scholastic Professional Books

Twinkle, Twinkle Little Star

Rewrite each sentence using periods.

1. Tonight I saw a star

_____

_____

2. I saw the star twinkle

_____

_____

3. It looked like a candle

_____

_____

4. It was very bright

_____

_____

5. I made a wish

_____

_____

6. I hope it comes true

_____

_____

Look for the brightest star in the sky. Make a wish. On another piece of paper, write a sentence about your wish.

Scholastic Professional Books

Hop to It!

 A **telling sentence** *begins with a* **capital letter** *and ends with a* **period.**

Rewrite each sentence correctly.

1. frogs and toads lay eggs

_____

_____

2. the eggs are in the water

_____

_____

3. tadpoles hatch from the eggs

_____

_____

4. the tadpoles grow legs

_____

_____

5. the tadpoles lose their tails

_____

_____

Scholastic Professional Books

Hop to It Some More!

Rewrite each sentence correctly.

1. tadpoles become frogs or toads

_____

_____

2. frogs live near water

_____

3. toads live under bushes

_____

4. frogs have wet skin

_____

5. toads have bumpy skin

_____

_____

 On another piece of paper, write three sentences about a time that you saw a frog or toad. Make sure you use capital letters and periods correctly.

Patriotic Sentences

 *A **sentence** tells a complete idea. It should always make sense.*

Color the flag to show:

RED = sentence   WHITE = not a sentence

★ ★ ★ ★ ★ ★ ... (stars)	This is a flag.
	The flag
	The flag has stars.
	The stars
	The stars are white.
	The stripes
	The stripes are red.

And white
The stripes are white.
Blue part
The flag has a blue part.
There are
There are 50 stars.

 Color the star part of the flag with a blue crayon. Then on another piece of paper, write a complete sentence about your colorful flag.

Scholastic Professional Books

High-Flying Sentences

Color each flag that tells a complete thought. Leave the other flags blank.

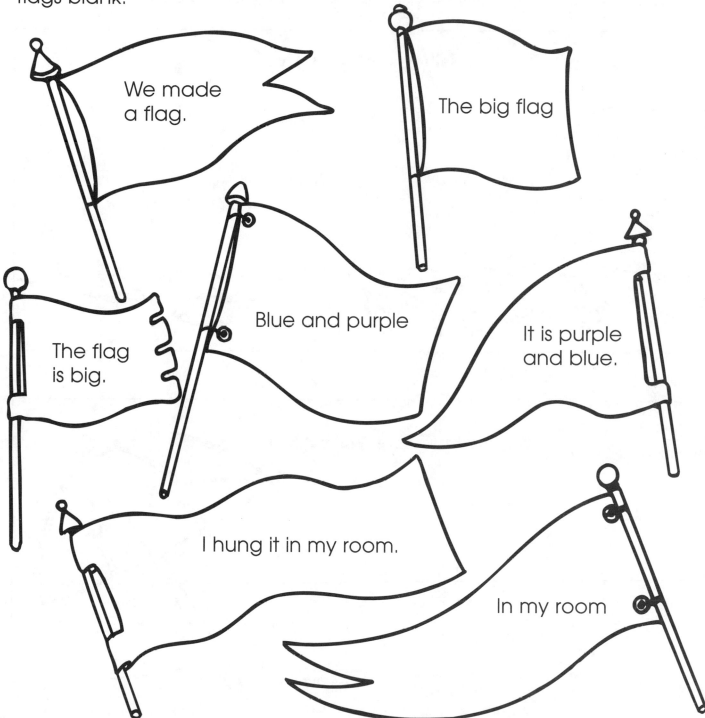

We made a flag.

The big flag

The flag is big.

Blue and purple

It is purple and blue.

I hung it in my room.

In my room

 On another piece of paper, turn this into a sentence: The biggest flag.

Scholastic Professional Books

At the Seashore

Unscramble the words to make a sentence. Write the new sentence below each picture. Finish each picture to match the sentence.

sailing are boats Five

four have We buckets

Scholastic Professional Books

In the Rain Forest

Unscramble the words to make a sentence. Write the new sentence. Do not forget to put a period at the end.

A hiding jaguar is

_____

- -

blue Some butterflies are

_____

- -

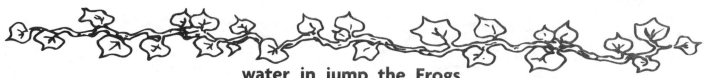

water in jump the Frogs

_____

- -

snakes trees Green hang from

_____

- -

very tall grow The trees

_____

- -

 Scramble a sentence for someone at home. Be sure the first word begins with a capital.

Scholastic Professional Books

Snakes Alive!

 *A sentence has a **naming part**. It tells who or what the sentence is about.*

Color the snake that tells the naming part in each sentence below.

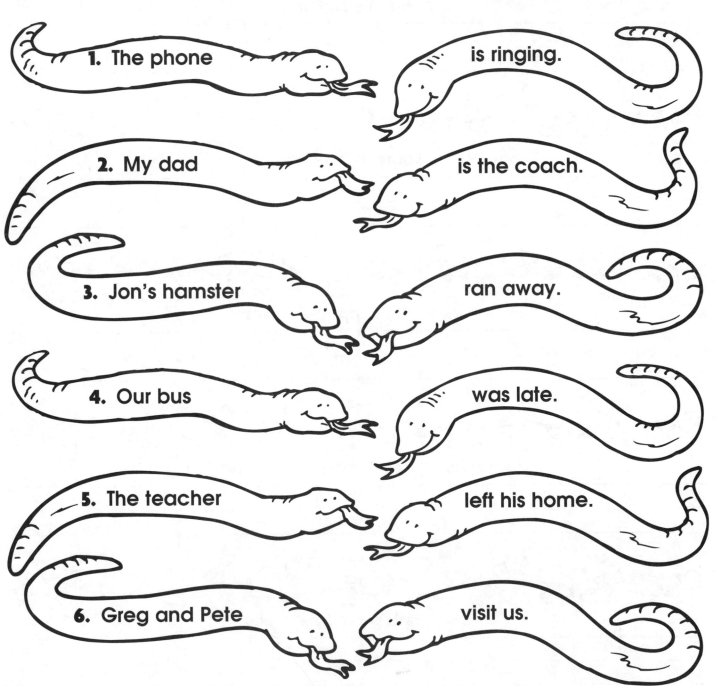

1. The phone   is ringing.

2. My dad   is the coach.

3. Jon's hamster   ran away.

4. Our bus   was late.

5. The teacher   left his home.

6. Greg and Pete   visit us.

On another piece of paper, write one of the sentences using a different naming part.

Scholastic Professional Books

Slithering Sentences

Circle the naming part in each sentence below.
Then color the picture to match.

1. The blue snake is playing with a friend.

2. The yellow snake is climbing a tree.

3. The green snake hides under rocks.

4. The brown snake is swimming.

5. The red snake is hanging on a tree.

6. The purple snake sleeps in trees.

7. The black snake rests on a rock.

8. The orange snake is near an egg.

 **Look around you. On another piece of paper, write three people or things that could be the
naming part of a sentence.**

Who Is That?

 The naming part of a sentence can be a person.

Use the pictures to find naming parts to make each sentence complete.

_____

1. _____ fell on the ice.

_____

2. _____ won the race.

_____

3. _____ went inside the dark cave.

_____

4. _____ climbed the hill.

_____

5. _____ swam across the pool.

Scholastic Professional Books

Where Is That?

 The naming part of a sentence can be a place or a thing.

Use naming parts to complete each sentence that tells about the map.

1. _____ is near the swings.

2. _____ is far from the cave.

3. _____ is a good place to fish.

4. _____ has bats inside.

5. _____ is along Tree Lane.

 **Find the naming part of three sentences in your favorite book.**

Family Photos

 The naming part of a sentence can be a person, a place, or a thing.

Use your own naming parts to write a complete sentence about each picture.

_____

- -

_____

_____

_____

- -

_____

_____

Scholastic Professional Books

More Family Photos

Use your own naming parts to write a complete sentence about each picture.

_____

- -

_____

_____

- -

_____

- -

_____

_____

- -

 Look at your family pictures. On another piece of paper, write a sentence telling about two of them.

Scholastic Professional Books

No Bones About It!

 *A sentence has an **action part**. It tells what is happening.*

Color the bone that tells the action part in each sentence below.

1. The dog   chases the cat.

2. The dog   hides the bone.

3. The dog   plays with a ball.

4. The dog   jumps in the air.

5. The dog   eats a bone.

6. The dog   sleeps on a rug.

 On another piece of paper, rewrite your favorite sentence.

Scholastic Professional Books

Mighty Good Sentences

Choose the ending that tells what each dog is doing. Remember to use periods.

is eating.

is sleeping.

is jumping.

is barking.

1. The white dog _____
_____

2. The gray dog _____

3. The spotted dog _____
_____

4. The striped dog _____

 On another piece of paper, draw another dog and write a sentence about it.

Scholastic Professional Books

Name _____

A Busy Classroom

 *The action part of a sentence is called the **verb**.*

Complete each sentence with an action verb to tell what is happening in the picture. Remember to use periods.

1. Mr. Downs _____

_____

2. The fish _____

_____

3. James _____

_____

4. Cara _____

 On another piece of paper, write a sentence about your teacher. Circle the action word.

Name _____

Pencil It In

 *Sometimes the verb does not show action.
It still tells what is happening.*

For example: I  the answer.

I am hungry.

Word Bank

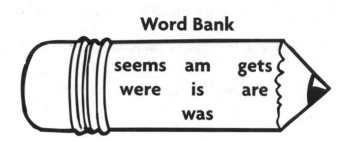

seems   am   gets
were   is   are
was

Choose a verb from the Word Bank
to complete each sentence.

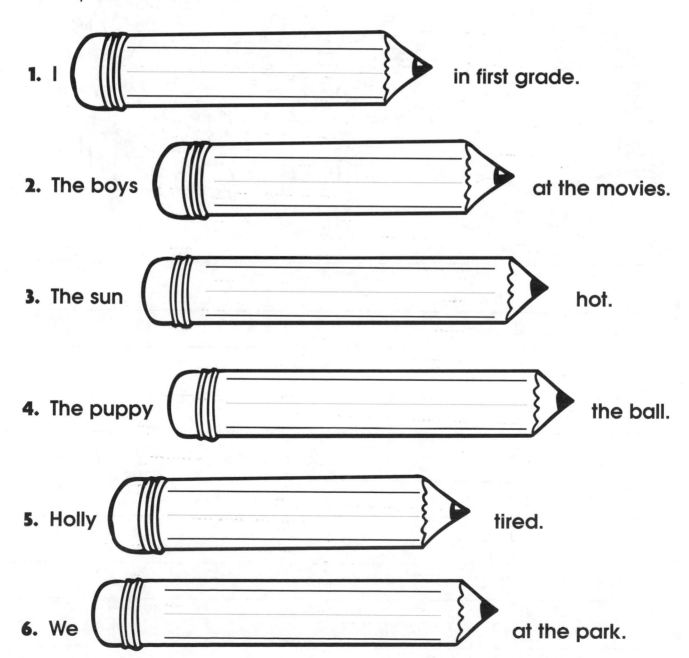

1. I _____ in first grade.

2. The boys _____ at the movies.

3. The sun _____ hot.

4. The puppy _____ the ball.

5. Holly _____ tired.

6. We _____ at the park.

Scholastic Professional Books

Topsy-Turvy!

 A sentence has a verb that tells what is happening.

Write five silly sentences that tell what is happening in the pictures.

_____

1. _____

_____

2. _____

_____

3. _____

_____

4. _____

_____

5. _____

Scholastic Professional Books

What Is Going On?

Look around you. Write four sentences that tell what is happening.

_____

1. _____

_____

_____

_____

2. _____

_____

_____

_____

3. _____

_____

_____

_____

4. _____

_____

_____

_____

 Find five action words in your favorite book. Write them on another piece of paper.

Scholastic Professional Books

The Caboose

 *A sentence is more interesting when it tells **where** the action is happening.*

In each caboose, draw a picture to show where each sentence takes place.

1. The plane flew into the clouds.

2. The princess played in the castle.

3. The boys fished in the lake.

Scholastic Professional Books

Chugging Along

Write an ending for each sentence that tells where the action takes place.

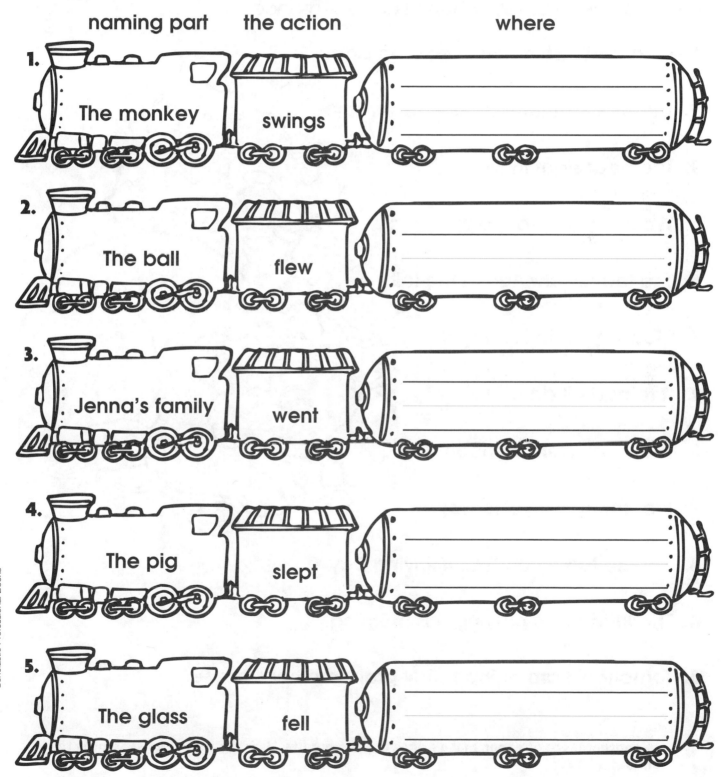

naming part   the action   where

1. The monkey swings

2. The ball flew

3. Jenna's family went

4. The pig slept

5. The glass fell

Scholastic Professional Books

When Was That?

➡️ *A sentence may also tell* **when** *the action takes place.*

Circle the part that tells when in each sentence.

1. George Washington lived long ago.

2. The mail carrier was late yesterday.

3. The bear slept in winter.

4. We are going to the zoo today.

5. The leaves change in the fall.

6. I lost my tooth last night.

7. It rained all day.

8. The party starts at noon.

9. We got home yesterday.

10. We ate turkey on Thanksgiving Day.

11. The kitten was playing this morning.

12. Tomorrow I am going to my grandmother's house.

 On another piece of paper, make a time line of your life. Use it to write two sentences that tell when.

Scholastic Professional Books

My Busy Day

 *Part of a sentence may tell **when** the action happened.*

Write the beginning part of each sentence to tell about your day.
Draw a picture to match each sentence.

this morning.

this afternoon.

tonight.

 On another piece of paper, write four sentences and draw four pictures to tell about your best day ever.

Scholastic Professional Books

Silly Sentences

 A sentence may have three parts: a naming part, an action, and a part that tells where or when.

Complete each missing part to make silly sentences.

the naming part	the action	where or when
1. The monkey		on his head.
2. My dad	is hopping	
3.	flipped	in the forest.
4. The ball	bounced	
5. My shoes		at the pool.
6. The snake	twisted	
7. The bubbles	filled	

 On another piece of paper, write a new sentence by scrambling three parts listed above. For example, use the naming part from #1, the action part from #2, and where or when from #3. Draw a picture of your sentence.

Scholastic Professional Books

Sweet Sentences

Use choices from each part to make three "sweet" sentences.

naming part	action	where or when
I	ate doughnuts	at the bakery
She	ate candy	at the party
He	chewed gum	at the circus

 On another piece of paper, name the three parts of this sentence: The doughnut shop closed at noon.

Scholastic Professional Books

Home Sweet Home

Write three sentences about the picture. For example: The dog is sleeping outside.

1. _____

_____

_____

2. _____

_____

_____

3. _____

_____

_____

Scholastic Professional Books

The Construction Crew

Write three sentences about the picture. Include three parts in each sentence.

1. _____
_____
_____

2. _____
_____
_____

3. _____
_____
_____

Scholastic Professional Books

Mystery Boxes

 Describing words help you imagine how something looks, feels, smells, sounds, or tastes.

Read the describing words to guess the mystery object. Use the Word Bank to help you.

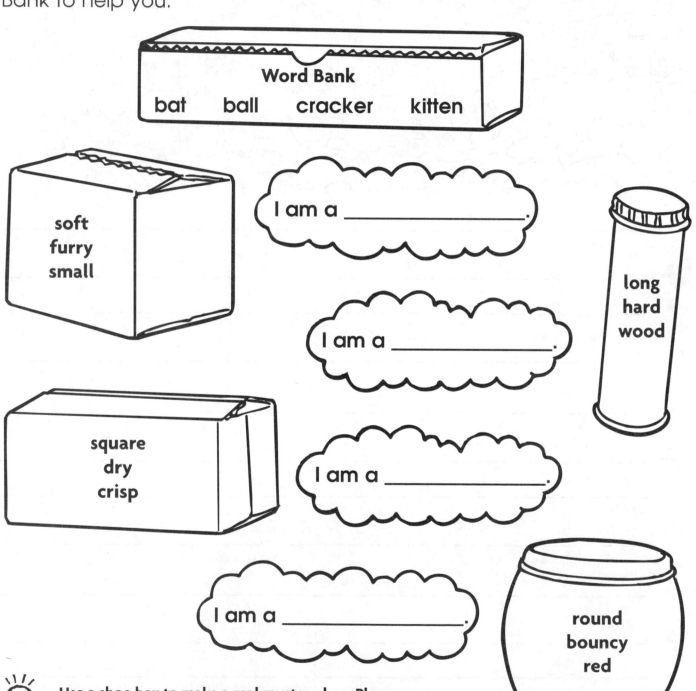

Word Bank

bat   ball   cracker   kitten

**soft
furry
small**

I am a _____.

**long
hard
wood**

I am a _____.

**square
dry
crisp**

I am a _____.

I am a _____.

**round
bouncy
red**

 Use a shoe box to make a real mystery box. Place an object inside and give describing clues to someone at home. Can he or she guess what's in the box?

Scholastic Professional Books

Sensational Words

Choose words from the Word Bank to describe each picture.

It tastes _____.

It looks _____.

It feels _____.

Word Bank

bumpy

crunchy

furry

gray

red

salty

smooth

squeaky

sweet

It feels _____.

It tastes _____.

It sounds _____.

It looks _____.

It sounds _____.

It feels _____.

Find two objects outside. On another piece of paper, write two adjectives to describe each object.

Scholastic Professional Books

Pretty Packages

 The describing words in a sentence help the reader paint a picture in his or her mind.

Write three words to describe each gift. Then color them to match.

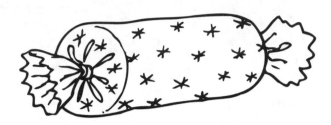

_____ (color)

_____ (color)

_____ (pattern)

_____ (color)

_____ (color)

_____ (pattern)

_____ (color)

_____ (color)

_____ (pattern)

_____ (color)

_____ (color)

_____ (pattern)

 Describe a "mystery object" to a friend. Can he or she guess what you are describing?

Scholastic Professional Books

What's Inside?

Use the describing words from page 38 to write a sentence about each package. For example: I found a swimsuit in the **yellow square** box.

1. I found _____ **in the**

_____

_____ **package.**

2. I found _____

_____ **in the**

_____ **package.**

3. I found _____ **in the**

_____

_____ **package.**

4. I found _____

_____ **in the**

_____ **package.**

Scholastic Professional Books

A Walk in the Park

➡️ *Describing words make a sentence more interesting.*

Write describing words to finish each sentence.

_____

1. A _____ duck is

swimming in the _____ pond.

_____

2. A _____ man is walking

his _____ dog.

_____

3. A _____ girl is

flying a _____ kite.

_____

4. A _____ woman is sitting

on a _____ .

 **On another piece of paper, draw a picture of your favorite animal at the zoo.
Then write two words to describe this animal.**

Scholastic Professional Books

Around Town

Write a sentence for each picture. Use the describing word in the sentence.

large

beautiful

crowded

noisy

On another piece of paper, write five words that describe your street.

Scholastic Professional Books

Keep It in Order

 Sentences can be written in order to tell a story.

Finish each story by writing sentences about the last pictures.

1. **First,** the spider crawls up

   Next, _____

   _____

   Last, _____

2. **First,** there is a tadpole

   Next, _____

   _____

   Last, _____

Scholastic Professional Books

What's Next?

 Sentences can be written in order to give directions.

Finish each set of directions by writing sentences about the last pictures.

1. First, mix all the ingredients

Next, _____

_____

Last, _____

2. First, put your dog in the tub

Next, _____

_____

Last, _____

Scholastic Professional Books

Which Title Fits?

 *The name of a story is called the **title**. It matches with the story. Most of the words in a title begin with capital letters.*

Match each title with its story. Write the title above the picture.

A Big Beak	The Big Win
My Space Friend	A Knight's Tale

_____
(title)

_____
(title)

_____
(title)

_____
(title)

Scholastic Professional Books

A Terrific Title

Fill in the missing words to make your own story. Then write a title that fits with your story. Draw a picture about your story in the box.

_____
(title)

One _____ day,

_____ took his pet

_____ for a walk. First,

they went to the _____.

Then they walked to _____'s

house. Last, they went home to _____

_____. It was a

_____ day!

Scholastic Professional Books

Story Strips

A story has a beginning, middle, and end.

Write a sentence to tell about each part of the story. Remember to give the story a title.

Beginning

_____
(title)

Middle

End

Scholastic Professional Books

More Story Strips

 A story has a beginning, middle, and end.

Think of a story you know well. Write about the beginning, middle, and end parts. Draw pictures to match. Be sure to give your story a title.

_____
(title)

Beginning

_____

Middle

_____

End

_____

 Fold a piece of paper two times to make a storybook. Write a story and draw pictures to match. Do not forget to write a title for your story.

Scholastic Professional Books

Page 4

The	For	That	with	know	but
here	on	When	Have	next	we
as	after	good	Make	there	see
Go	Look	Are	Could	is	why
This	who	said	in	come	them
Has	Name	Before	Her	Where	Th

Page 5
1. The mouse; 2. He finds;
3. He eats; 4. Then he;
5. Oh no!; 6. The mouse

Page 6
1. We read; 2. Then we;
3. My bed; 4. My cat;
5. The sky; 6. My eyes

Page 7
1. My dog; 2. She must;
3. Maybe she;
4. Sometimes she; 5. I think

Page 8
Check that the child has added a period to the end of each sentence.

Page 9
Check that the child has added a period to the end of each sentence.

Page 10
1. Frogs and toads lay eggs. 2. The eggs are in the water. 3. Tadpoles hatch from the eggs.
4. The tadpoles grow legs.
5. The tadpoles lose their tails.

Page 11
1. Tadpoles become frogs or toads. 2. Frogs live near water. 3. Toads live under bushes. 4. Frogs have wet skin. 5. Toads have bumpy skin.

Page 12
The following sentences should be colored red: This is a flag., The flag has stars., The stars are white., The stripes are red., The stripes are white., The flag has a blue part., There are 50 stars.; The rest are not sentences and should be colored white.

Page 13

Page 14
Five boats are sailing.; We have four buckets.

Page 15
A jaguar is hiding.; Some butterflies are blue.; Frogs jump in the water.; Green snakes hang from trees.; The trees grow very tall.

Page 16
The snakes on the left side of the page should have been colored.

Page 17
1. The blue snake;
2. The yellow snake;
3. The green snake;
4. The brown snake;
5. The red snake; 6. The purple snake; 7. The black snake; 8. The orange snake

Page 18
Sentences will vary.

Page 19
Sentences will vary.

Page 20
Sentences will vary.

Page 21
Sentences will vary.

Page 22
The bones on the right side of the page should have been colored.

Page 23
1. is jumping.; 2. is barking.; 3. is eating.;
4. is sleeping.

Page 24
Sentences will vary.

Page 25
Answers will vary.

Page 26
Sentences will vary.

Page 27
Sentences will vary.

Page 28
Pictures will vary.

Page 29
Answers will vary.

Page 30
1. long ago; 2. yesterday;
3. in winter; 4. today; 5. in the fall; 6. last night; 7. all day; 8. at noon;
9. yesterday; 10. on Thanksgiving Day; 11. this morning; 12. Tomorrow

Page 31
Sentences will vary.

Page 32
Answers will vary.

Page 33
Sentences will vary.

Page 34
Sentences will vary.

Page 35
Sentences will vary.

Page 36
kitten, bat, cracker, ball

Page 37
sweet, red, smooth; bumpy, salty, crunchy,; small, squeaky, furry

Page 38
Adjectives will vary.

Page 39
Sentences will vary.

Page 40
Sentences will vary.

Page 41
Sentences will vary.

Page 42
Sentences will vary.

Page 43
Sentences will vary.

Page 44
My Space Friend; A Big Beak; The Big Win; A Knight's Tale

Page 45
Stories will vary.

Page 46
Sentences will vary.

Page 47
Sentences and pictures will vary.

Scholastic Professional Books